A SPIRIT DAUGHTER WORKBOOK

WRITTEN BY
JILL WINTERSTEEN

FOR VIRGO SEASON
AUGUST 22 – SEPTEMBER 22

THE NEW MOON
MONDAY, SEPTEMBER 6TH, 2021
5:51PM PDT

PGS. 2-15: VIRGO SEASON
PGS. 16-27: VIRGO NEW MOON
PGS. 28-29: VIRGO SIGN INFO
PGS. 30-31: ASTROLOGY FORECAST

VIRGO

From the fires of Leo Season and the eclectic nature of two Aquarius Full Moons, we meet Virgo. Ruled by Earth, Virgo Season ushers in a period of transition as we move from summer to fall and feel our energy settle and refine. This period gives us a foundation to rest upon as we process the events of summer. It allows us to organize our lives after the chaotic burst of energy Leo Season often brings. The past four weeks gave us time to define and feel who we really are in this world. Virgo Season brings us an opportunity to show up as that person and realize our inherent self-worth. It is a time to let go of self-doubt, perfectionism, and self-criticism as we step into our potential in this lifetime. Virgo's energy helps us embrace our authentic self and accept it with compassion, forgiveness, and strength.

It does not matter whether you have Virgo predominantly in your chart or not. Virgo Season helps everyone see their potential. This season shows us who we could be if we allow ourselves to fully step into our power. It is also a time to find balance between who we could become and who we are right now. Virgo reminds us that if we are always comparing ourselves to our ideal version, then we will never experience true joy. On the other hand, if we stop growing and striving to become a better version of ourselves, then we stagnate and become unhappy, or worse. We must find balance between accepting ourselves as is and wanting to transform into the next version of ourselves. The question of the season becomes: How can you love and accept yourself today while working to become your future self?

The first step in accepting yourself as you are today is letting go of conditions you must meet for love and acceptance. We often hold ourselves to an impossible standard, and when we fail to meet it, we fall prey to shame, embarrassment, self-doubt, and should-ing ourselves. We tend to hide our mistakes and mull them over, forgetting that others love us and want to support us. We feel that we are the only ones going through something and that everyone else has their life together far better than we do. We also compare ourselves to others without even knowing

VIRGO

them or understanding their struggles. We often tell ourselves that we have to meet certain criteria to be loved by others or to love ourselves. We may even judge our worth on what we do, not who we are.

As we journey through Virgo Season, become aware of the conditions you place on yourself for love and acceptance. What impossible level of perfectionism are you holding yourself to and why? We often feel that we have to be perfect to receive love and be worthy. Over this season, began to teach yourself that you are worthy of love, acceptance, and fulfilled dreams just as you are right now. You do not have to do anything more than what you are doing right now. Begin by embracing all aspects of yourself this season. Purge your consciousness of unworthiness at the beginning of Virgo Season by making a list of all the reasons why you don't believe you deserve love, belonging, acceptance, or fulfilled dreams. Write unrestricted and break free of the bonds of shame that keep you tied to a life of self-doubt. What don't you feel you are good enough for? What in your past or present is preventing you from owning your magic and declaring your worth to the Universe?

Letting go of these things that make you feel unworthy can be a long process. Allow this season to start you on the road of accepting your worth and cultivating a life that is full of everything you deserve. You deserve love, you deserve joy, and you deserve to have in your life people who accept you for who you are today. These are not things you need to jump through hoops for. Rather, they are your birthright as a human. You may have been taught differently growing up, and perhaps you were given conditions that you had to meet to earn love and acceptance. But that is not the way you have to live. It may take work to get there, but you can heal yourself and realize that your self-worth as a person does not depend on anything other than you being yourself. It all starts with a deep self-acceptance and appreciation despite any experiences that may have caused you to feel pain, shame, or unworthiness. What do you need to heal this Virgo Season to begin to feel your worth and know you are good enough?

Healing is at the heart of Virgo's energy. This season is a time to heal the places in you that feel unloved. It's a time to write yourself love letters about all the wonderful gifts you have to give the world, and a time to have compassion for yourself. It's also a time to define your boundaries both with yourself and others. Healing is often linked to boundaries. You must be willing to say yes to the things that matter and no—without guilt—to the things that feed your insecurity or sense of scarcity. Some of the boundaries will be with yourself, including your thoughts and your habits. Others will be with friends, colleagues, and other partners. Align with the Earth element this season to feel where you need boundaries, then know you are worthy of upholding them. You are worthy of the healing that strong boundaries provide.

Many of the boundaries created in Virgo Season can help you carve out time to work on yourself, your healing, and your worth. When you have a set time to work on yourself each day, it becomes easier to find balance between who you are and who you could be. You can accept yourself as you are while knowing you have time and space to become your next version. Over this season, align with the organizational energy of Virgo to create a schedule or routine of healing and growth. This may look like taking a class or reading a new book. It may be making time to meditate or journal each morning. It might be weekly acupuncture or yoga classes, or some other healing modality that serves you. The key is to give yourself permission and time to evolve while knowing you are still worthy of everything you desire right now. Work on yourself because you can and because it's enjoyable to grow, not because it's required for you to be good enough. You're already good enough.

MOONSCOPES

Your Moon sign is the astrological sign the Moon was positioned in when you were born. It rules your emotional body and can give clues to what you need to feel fulfilled. Below is advice on your Moon sign and emotional body is affected by the energy of Virgo. They also tell where to look for opportunities for growth this season.

Aries Moon: You are full of fire and have a determined heart. You seek experiences that require courage, and you never back down from a chance to grow. Over Virgo Season, learn to love and accept yourself in the moment. Slow down a bit and realize that not all situations require you to charge full steam ahead; some ask that you pause and feel your feet on the ground. On the New Moon, ask yourself how you can bring your passion for life to your craft. Then be courageous in giving your gifts to others, helping them find just as much passion for life as you have.

Taurus Moon: You align well this Virgo Season, as you are both ruled by the Earth. You need to feel your feet on the ground and know that you have something to stand upon. This security helps you take leaps and share yourself fully with the world. It also helps you let of go of self-doubts and feel your worth. Over Virgo Season, find ways to elevate your self-worth and praise yourself for being who you are right now. Find security in loving and accepting yourself without the approval of anyone else. On the New Moon, let go of fears around not being good enough and realize that the world is awaiting your many talents.

Gemini Moon: You and Virgo share the planetary ruler Mercury. On an intellectual level, you pair all with this season. It feels good to you, and you embrace the many gifts this season has to offer. Be cautious to not overthink things this season or get lost in your anxiety about the future. Lean into being more than doing, and feeling more than thinking. You already know all the answers; you don't need to seek anywhere else except within your own energy. On the New Moon, focus your sharp mind on one intention to work with this cycle. Yes, there are many energies trying to grab your attention, but committing to one will give you the best opportunity for growth.

Cancer Moon: You share a deep feminine nature and brilliant intuition with Virgo. Feel into the gifts of intuition this season. Work on your ability to receive answers and knowledge when you need them most. Feel your power in this world and know that you do not have to do anything to be worthy of it. Your strength is in your softness. You do not need to fix anything about yourself; you only need to accept and embrace every part of yourself. On the New Moon, set intentions that include your greatest power—your intuition. It is your gift, and you can use it to help heal yourself and the world.

Leo Moon: You are on a journey this lifetime to accept yourself and embrace your talents. You were born with a greater capacity to love than most people have, and your gift is to show others how to love. Over Virgo Season, model how to lead your life with your heart. Have compassion for yourself and forgive yourself for your mistakes. You do not need to be perfect to be loved. You only need to be yourself. On the New Moon, set intentions that include living with an open heart. If every choice you made was made with love and acceptance, what would life look like?

Virgo Moon: You enjoy being of service to others, and it fulfills you. The first step in giving to others, however, is to believe you are good enough. Over Virgo Season, feel into your strengths and honor them. Know that you are appreciated for your talents and give them freely to others—not for praise, but for the satisfaction of helping another. Also, feel your intuition guiding you even more strongly this season. Let it bring you answers in the most unexpected ways. On the New Moon, set intentions that create a life free of self-criticism. Notice how free you feel without the weight of perfectionism on you. What will you do with this freedom?

*You can look up your personal moon sign at astro-charts.com

MOONSCOPES

Libra Moon: Your heart needs harmony and balance. Much of your work this lifetime is to create peace throughout your life, which means experiencing things that give you an opportunity to find what calms your spirit. Over Virgo Season, notice what in you needs healing for you to feel peace in your heart. What tools can help you create calmness, and how much time do you need to give yourself to work with these tools? Over this season, create routines that nourish you and restore balance. On the New Moon, set intentions to understand that you may not always feel calm but you are still worthy of the life you desire. You do not need to be a perfect picture of harmony, but you can work toward it while loving yourself in the moment.

Scorpio Moon: You are here to feel everything and understand the mystery of life. You never fear a path of transformation, and you embrace every step of your evolution. Virgo Season is a time for you to love yourself in the state you are right now. Yes, you can always grow and shift, but there is power in standing still for a moment and accepting yourself today. Over this season, look back at how far you've come and feel into how worthy you are of this moment. Feel how this acceptance is healing and how healing will elevate you to the next level. On the New Moon, set intentions around how you can share your gifts of insight and transformation with others. You tend to keep your talents to yourself. Feel how the world needs them and make plans to share them with others.

Sagittarius Moon: You love to explore, go on adventures, and evolve. Your heart is constantly craving new experiences that teach you the unexpected. Virgo Season can feel a bit restrictive and limiting to you. Notice if you feel restlessness with this energy, and instead of running away from these feelings, explore them. Settle down for a moment and reflect on what you've learned in your lifetime. Develop the gifts you already have and find ways to share them with others. Realize that you already know enough and that, while learning new things is wonderful, you can rest in your knowledge right now. On the New Moon, feel into your natural joy and optimism when setting intentions. Create a vision of yourself and your life that assumes the best will happen.

Capricorn Moon: Your heart needs a mission, and you often find one in your work. Over Virgo Season, feel the abundance of Earth energy helping you focus on what matters most in your life. Just remember to take a break when you need it and appreciate all the work you have done. You do not need to do anything to be worthy of love and acceptance. Ensure you are working hard at your mission because it fulfills you, not because you need validation. On the New Moon, set intentions that incorporate your determination and your need to make a difference in this world. You are capable of great things if you take care of yourself in the process of creating them.

Aquarius Moon: Your heart wants to be of service to the world and help it evolve. Virgo Season brings out this need and helps you refine it. You are full of ideas and concepts that move society forward. You just need to know they are worthy and needed by others. You may not be accepted at first by everybody, but that is ok. Over this season, feel into your inherent gifts of seeing the world in unique ways. Make them the center of your messages and from here, organize a plan to help lead the world to a new place. On the New Moon, set intentions that encourage you to speak your truth and know that it is good enough for the world to hear.

Pisces Moon: You are a natural healer and have the capacity to feel more than others. Over Virgo Season, feel your inherent gifts of healing and know that they can be of great service. You are highly empathetic and have the ability to feel what others are feeling. Over Virgo Season, learn to discern which emotions are yours and which belong to other people. Then learn how to release what is not yours. Once you feel comfortable taking on others' emotions and releasing them with ease, you will deepen your healing ability. On the New Moon, set intentions that offer you a path to show up as a powerful healer. Know that you will feel many intense energies, but you can handle them all.

CRYSTALS FOR VIRGO

Smokey Quartz is a wonderful stone for grounding and releasing negativity. It will help you rid yourself of unwanted feelings, including anxiety and perfectionism. Hold it when you feel your mind begin to criticize and critique, as these are the lower vibrations of Virgo Season. Have a piece near you while you meditate to ground your energy and help you feel connected to the Earth. It will stabilize and strengthen your energetic field while sending any lower frequencies back to the Earth to be recycled.

Smokey Quartz vibrates to the mantra: "I am grounded."

Dumortierite brings both patience and the will to stand your ground. Its vibration centers your energy and clarifies your vision. It helps you understand who you are and how to take control of your life by believing in yourself. It also helps you access your psychic visions and intuition. Hold a piece when you feel confused or overwhelmed by information and need to access your inner knowledge to make a decision. If the external world is drawing too much of your attention, place a piece in your pocket to stay grounded and centered on yourself.

Dumortierite vibrates to the mantra: "I am clear."

Pink Calcite is a stone of self-love and self-acceptance. It will assist you in loving every part of yourself and feeling your inherent worth. It also helps direct energy away from negative vibrations of fear, anxiety, and nervousness that can come with the low side of Virgo's energy. It is a wonderful stone if you need to return to your inner home to raise your self-worth and trust in yourself. Hold a piece while meditating when you need to let go of self-criticism and heal yourself with love.

Pink Calcite vibrates to the mantra: "I accept myself."

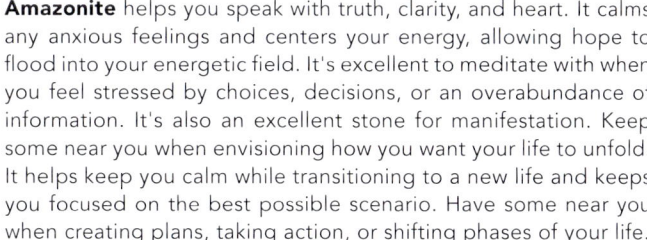

Amazonite helps you speak with truth, clarity, and heart. It calms any anxious feelings and centers your energy, allowing hope to flood into your energetic field. It's excellent to meditate with when you feel stressed by choices, decisions, or an overabundance of information. It's also an excellent stone for manifestation. Keep some near you when envisioning how you want your life to unfold. It helps keep you calm while transitioning to a new life and keeps you focused on the best possible scenario. Have some near you when creating plans, taking action, or shifting phases of your life.

Amazonite vibrates to the mantra: "I am calm."

Unakite brings you in touch with your psychic visions and intuition. It can even bring them to you while you sleep by calming any anxious vibrations that come up in the night. Place a piece under your pillow so you have a calming night's sleep and awaken with a knowledge of the future. It can also help clear attachments to old habits and ways of thinking or being. If you feel something is holding you back from pursuing your dreams with full commitment, look to this stone to free you. Hold some while meditating to help move your energy forward in a new direction, guided by your intuition.

Unakite vibrates to the mantra: "I see."

VIRGO MEDITATION

Earthing + Walking Meditation

Earthing is a practice of connecting with the Earth and harnessing its frequency to balance your energy. We have become disconnected from the Earth due to shoes, the homes we live in, and the cars we drive. For centuries humans walked barefoot on the Earth, and our energetic bodies still crave this connection for restoration and balance. Over Virgo Season and on her New Moon, find an area in nature where you feel comfortable walking around in bare feet. Allow the Earth's energy to bring harmony to your system and ground your vibration, leaving you restored and clear minded.

Earthing is a simple technique. Find an area where you can safely connect with the Earth, then take off your shoes. Before beginning, firmly press the Kidney One acupuncture point. Find this point on the sole of your foot, about a third of the way down from your second toe. When activated through pressure or acupuncture, this point connects us to the infinite energy of the Earth. It also grounds our energy, restoring balance to our system. Press this point on each foot for about fifteen seconds. Then place your feet on the ground, observing the sensation of your bare feet on the Earth. Feel the texture of the Earth as you wiggle your toes in the soil or sand. Feel the temperature of the Earth and even her density as you allow yourself to sink in and be supported by Mother Nature.

Close your eyes to bring even more focus to the sensations in your feet. Clear your mind and focus on your breath as you continue to connect your feet to the Earth. Allow your breath to help anchor and steady your mind. Say to yourself, "I am inhaling" as you inhale, and "I am exhaling" as you exhale. Feel the Earth's energy drawing up through the Kidney One point on each inhale, like roots drawing up water. Then feel your connection with the ground strengthening on each exhale. You may even feel the surface of your feet expand on each exhale, helping enhance your connection.

Keeping your eyes closed, add some movement to your body. Slowly shift your weight to your right foot as you inhale, then pause for the exhale. Shift your weight to your left foot on the inhale, pausing here for the exhale. Continue playing with your weight for about 10 breaths, then stand still with both feet firmly on the ground. Open your eyes while staying deeply aware of your feet and the ground beneath you.

Begin to walk on the Earth slowly. You can have a designated path, or you can walk freely. Continue to be mindful of your breath as you walk, inhaling as you lift your foot and exhaling as you place it down. On each exhale, allow your full weight to land on the ground, feeling the Earth supporting you. As you lift each foot, still feel the opposite foot's connection on the ground, maintaining your relationship with the Earth. Continue walking like this for 10 to 15 minutes. Make your movements slow and purposeful, as if you were learning how to walk for the first time. If your mind begins to wander, come back to your breath and the sensations occurring on the soles of your feet.

After you've completed your walk, stop and stand. Close your eyes and feel centered through your body and with the Earth. Feel the energy of the ground circulating through your body, restoring it and bringing your entire system into balance. Give gratitude to the Earth for supporting you as she has done your entire life. Also, thank yourself for taking this time to connect with nature.

You can practice this earthing and walking meditation at any time. You can even practice it in the rain to add new sensations and elements. Return to it anytime you feel drained, anxious, or disconnected from your intuition. This practice and Mother Earth are always available to support you on your journey.

VIRGO LUNAR FLOW

Virgo rules our digestive and nervous systems. The following sequence is designed to address these areas of your body by bringing fluidity to your energy and decreasing the nervous tension Virgo's energy often causes. You can practice this sequence throughout Virgo Season and on her New Moon. Please modify any poses for your body and vibration.

Begin by lying on your mat. Bring your awareness to your breath and count to 4 on the inhale and 4 on the exhale. Do this for 10 breaths before starting, and continue this equanimous breathing through the entire sequence.

Supine Crescent Moon Pose
While still lying down, stretch your arms overhead and bend your body to the right in the shape of a Crescent Moon, with both hips firmly on the ground. Lightly grab your left wrist and cross your right ankle over your left. Take 5 breaths here. Then switch sides for 5 breaths.

Knee-to-Chest Pose
Still lying on the ground, hug your right knee into your chest and take 5 breaths. Switch sides for 5 breaths, then hug both knees into your body.

Boat Pose
Still holding both knees into your chest, inhale and lift your nose to your knees. Then release your arms, extending them alongside your feet. On your exhale, stretch your legs outward for Boat Pose. On your next exhale, try to pike up to balancing on your sit bones in a V shape; you can bend your knees if needed. Take 5 breaths and release to a Cross-Seated Pose.

Seated Twist
From a crossed-legged position, exhale and twist to the right. Place your left hand on your right knee and your right hand behind you. On each inhale, expand through your chest and grow taller; on each exhale, twist a little more deeply. Continue for 5 breaths, then switch sides for another 5 breaths.

Standing Forward Bend
Roll forward from a seated position to your feet and fold forward over your body. Allow your knees to bend slightly so your torso can rest on the top of your thighs. Catch the opposite elbows with your hands and relax here, lengthening through your spine, for 5 to 10 breaths. When finished, slowly roll up to standing.

Sun Salutation A
Start by standing on the top of your mat. Inhale and stretch your arms overhead. Exhale and fold forward. Inhale, lengthen out your back. Exhale, step back into Plank Pose and lower to the ground. Inhale, reach your chest up for Cobra Pose, legs staying on the ground. Exhale, stretch back to Downward Dog Pose. Stay here for 5 breaths and feel your entire body expand. On exhale, step back to the top of the mat. Inhale, lengthen out through your spine. Exhale, fold forward. Inhale, come up to standing, reaching your arms overhead. Exhale, return your hands to your heart. Pause for a moment and feel centered on the ground and through your body. Repeat this sequence three times.

VIRGO LUNAR FLOW

Warrior 2 > Reverse Warrior > Triangle > Wide-Legged Forward Bend
Step your feet about 3 to 4 feet apart on your mat, facing the right side of your mat, with your feet parallel. Turn your left foot to face the front of your mat, your right foot turning in slightly. Extend your arms out to either side and bend your left knee into Warrior 2. Breathe here for 5 breaths and feel the strength of your legs supporting you. On inhale, flip your left palm up to the sky, exhale, and stretch back into Reverse Warrior for 5 breaths. Elongate through your left-side waist. Inhale, lift your torso back up, and straighten your left leg. Exhale, extend from your torso—reaching forward—and place your left hand on the ground on the outside of your left foot or shin, then rotate your torso to the right. Stretch and reach upward through your right arm, feeling one long line of energy from fingertip to fingertip. Take 5 full breaths here, feeling your weight evenly on both feet. On inhale, lift your torso back up and bring your feet to parallel. Place your hands on your hips, take a deep inhale, reach your chest up, and fold forward on your exhale. Release your hands to the ground and allow your spine and neck to fully release, feeling supported by your legs. Take 5 breaths here. Place your hands back on your hips and slowly come up to standing. Rotate your right foot toward the back of the mat and practice the entire sequence on the other side.

Chair Pose > Standing-Forward Bend
Return to the front of your mat. Keep your feet together and bend deeply into your knees as if you were sitting in a chair. Reach your arms upward to the sky and look up. Feel your belly drawing in, helping direct your tailbone to the floor. Breathe here for 5 breaths and feel the strength of your legs. Inhale, come back up to standing, exhale, and fold forward for 5 breaths, allowing your torso to lengthen again. On inhale, slowly roll up to standing.

Ardha Matsyendrasana
Come to a seated position on your mat with your legs straight. Then bend your knees, placing your feet on the floor. Slide your right leg under your left one (which is still upright), placing your left foot by your right hip and laying your left leg on the ground. Tighten the pose by further crossing your left ankle over your right knee. Inhale, reach your left arm up to the sky, stretching your left-side waist. Exhale and twist to the right, either wrapping your arm around your left knee or hooking your right elbow around the side of your left leg with your palm facing left. Place your left hand behind yourself for support on the ground or on a block. Breathe here for 5 breaths, lengthening on each inhale and twisting deeper on each exhale.

Baddha Konasana
Come back to a neutral seated position and take the soles of your feet together, knees out to either side. Grab ahold of your feet and inhale as you lengthen through your spine. Exhale, fold over your legs, and breathe here for 5 to 10 minutes. Feel your inhales extend down into your hips, opening them, and your exhales relaxing your entire nervous system.

Savasana
Stretch both your legs out long on the mat and place your palms facing upward in a receptive position. Feel your entire body supported by the ground beneath you. Let your breath become natural and feel the energy circulating through you from your practice. Allow your mind to be still and your body to be calm.

ALIGNING THE SPIRIT

8 TIPS FOR OVERCOMING PERFECTIONISM

1. Begin
There is no perfect time to start something. When taking on new projects or new ways of being, we first must just begin. Often this is scary, as we feel the starting point is arbitrary. But actually, when we simply start something, without overanalyzing its timing, we flow directly from our intuition. We essentially do start at the perfect time; it's just not definable. Our instinct takes over and gives us the drive and motivation to begin. When we stop analyzing and worrying about the perfect moment, we unlock the part of us that instinctively knows the ideal time to begin. So don't over think it. When your gut tells you to start, then it's time.

2. Celebrate Every Victory
Life does not have to be perfect to be wonderful or celebrated. As you move through your journey, celebrate every victory, no matter how small. Perfectionism can often make us feel dissatisfied with what we have accomplished. We think it is never good enough, and we miss an opportunity to celebrate how far we've come. Take the time to acknowledge what you have accomplished each step of the way. Pat yourself on the back and thank yourself for what you've completed.

3. Don't Sweat the Small Stuff
See the bigger picture of your life and recognize that not all pieces need to be perfect for the puzzle to be beautiful. We often get caught in a trap of details that don't matter in the grand scheme of things. We overanalyze and nitpick as a way to fulfill our need for perfection, but in reality, we are wasting our precious energy.

ALIGNING THE SPIRIT

8 TIPS FOR OVERCOMING PERFECTIONISM

Yes, many things matter, but many other things don't. Learn to discern where to place your focus, and avoid spending time on the intricacies that don't contribute to the bigger picture.

4. Embrace Failures
Failures are powerful opportunities for growth and learning. Everyone fails at some point and are better off for the experience. The importance of failure lies in the lessons it teaches us. Instead of shaming or blaming yourself, try to view the failure as a positive event and extract the knowledge it provides. Failures show us information about ourselves. They teach us about pieces we haven't thought about before, and they shed light on how to work with the unknown. Failures ultimately give us a more in-depth understanding of ourselves, our project, and our energy. Learn to embrace failures and allow them to open doors into places you would not have reached otherwise.

5. Accept the Past
Fear of regret is one of the most significant pieces of perfectionism. We become so afraid of making a mistake and feeling regret that we fail to try anything at all. Often this fear is a result of a past mistake and the subsequent emotions that occurred afterward. We falsely believe that if we are perfect this time around, we won't have to feel regret. Learn to accept that everything unfolds at the right time in the right way, and sometimes this does not match our expectations. When our expectations are not met, we may feel we did something wrong. Trust that life is flowing in the best way possible, even if it appears to be not working in your favor. Accept the events of the past and don't allow them to hold you back from your future.

6. Balance Work and Life
The more we work, the more time we give ourselves for perfectionism. Schedule time for play, nourishment, and life outside work. Even if you initially resent taking time away from your work, the break will provide a new perspective and will help you not obsess over every detail. Don't let the pendulum swing the other way either, though, by depriving yourself of the time and effort you need to work on yourself or your projects. Find a balance between work and play. This balance will help you maintain a healthy relationship with yourself.

7. Avoid Comparison
Comparison is a road to nowhere. We can never compare ourselves to others because we are all unique snowflakes with our own life paths and energetic evolution. Comparison can fuel perfectionism because it creates an unobtainable goal. It makes us feel that we are not good enough because we can never be someone else. Learn to love yourself and your unique path. Find gratitude for your journey. Allow this love and gratitude to bring the focus back to yourself and your goals.

8. Accept Your Best + Ask for Help
Always try your best, but also accept your best. Most things in life don't need to be perfect. If they do require perfection, get help so that you are pulling together everyone's best attributes for the project. None of us are perfect alone, and it is futile to try. But together we can make something beautiful.

*be patient with yourself,
you are the magic
of the universe
unfolding at it's
own rhythm*

WHY THE NEW MOON?

SEPTEMBER 6TH

Dark Side of the Moon

The New Moon occurs every twenty-nine days and is known in astrology as a time of darkness in the lunar cycle. Darkness can be viewed in many ways. We often associate it with negativity or sadness. It is inherently neither—we just culturally place these attributes on it. It is more accurate to associate darkness with an inward pull of energy. Darkness is what we see when our eyes are closed in meditation or when we sleep. It denotes a time when the light and other energies are shut out from our consciousness. When we are in darkness, we are with ourselves and our unique energy. It becomes a personal time to travel inward and seek answers rather than look for answers in the external world.

Before the advent of electricity and portable light, the Moon played a major role in the activity of humans at night. When it was waxing to full or waning from full, people could go out at night and still have sight. As the Moon approached the New Moon or had just started waxing, sight was limited. So people chose to stay inside or near their camp, where there was fire for light. The natural cycle of the Moon influenced a natural cycle of behavior, with the New Moon providing a time to sit alone and contemplate questions. It was a time to formulate new ways of thinking without the disturbance of other people's energy. The bright side of the lunar cycle, around the Full Moon, was when these new ideas could be shared with others.

Although today we have the convenience of electricity, the New Moon and Dark Moon (a day before the New Moon) still energetically provide us with a period of contemplative darkness. It is during this time we can travel further inward to depths of the subconscious mind, and allow answers and ideas to float to the surface. Once they come into the conscious mind, we can shed light on them and bring them to fruition. We can manifest them in reality, but first we need become aware of them.

The information gathered in the darkness of the New Moon comes from intuition and the subconscious. It comes from the part of ourselves that we are unaware of—a part that controls us from behind the conscious mind. It is also the part that is connected to the knowledge of the Universe. Through the darkness of the New Moon, we can feel our true desires and write intentions around them. We can feel the subconscious blocks that prevent us from manifesting our dreams, and we can create ways to dissolve those blocks. We can also feel the psychic vision that informs our next steps. The New Moon is a time to trust ourselves and take leaps based in an inner knowing—leaps that lead us to the life we ultimately want to live.

Adding to the magic of the New Moon is a spark of energy that comes when the Moon and Sun meet in the sky in the same zodiac sign. This conjunction gives an energetic boost to our intentions and helps us make changes in our lives. The zodiac constellation flavors, or themes, the energy of the New Moon. It helps us focus and clarify our intentions, and points to what we need to work on to manifest our dreams. No matter what sign you may be, the qualities of that sign come through the cosmos and raise awareness in these areas of your life. The New Moon shows us places in our consciousness that are linked to the quality of the sign it inhabits, and we can work with those energies in our own life. Each New Moon brings us darkness, but with that darkness come insights, illuminations, and power guidance that help us shift our lives one Moon at a time.

VIRGO X NEW MOON

SEPTEMBER 6TH

FIND THE MAGIC WITHIN YOU, NOURISH IT, THEN HAVE THE COURAGE TO GIVE IT TO OTHERS

The Virgo New Moon brings form and detail to our intentions. It's a time to craft our visions with precision and know that the more direction we can give the Universe, the more it will give us in return. During this Moon you can become crystal clear on what you want and what you need to heal within yourself to get it. What in you needs acceptance, love, and nurturing for your visions to manifest? The Virgo New Moon helps you answer this question and many more so you can step into a life that allows you to fully show up as yourself.

Virgo's energy reminds us that each of us has a unique gift to give the world. We all can be of service in some way. This service will look different for each person, but it will have the same core definition. We each have something to offer that no one else on this planet can duplicate. The key is to find this piece of magic within, nourish it, then have the courage to give it to others. We must know that we—and our gifts—are good enough. We must also recognize that we are unique and that holding back our gift holds back the evolution of the world.

On this New Moon, feel into what you offer the collective. How can you be of service? And is there anything holding you back from contributing your skill or craft to others? The Virgo New Moon always asks you to release something, and that something is perfectionism. It asks that you examine all the ways you hide your talents out of fear that they are not worthy of the light of day. As you journey through this New Moon, make a list of what holds you back from stepping into your magic and allowing others to see your brilliance. What fears come up when you try to envision a life that includes sharing your gifts with others? Before writing your intentions, work on releasing anything that causes you self-doubt or makes you feel not good enough. As you release these blocks, you'll clear the pathway forward to creating a life in which you can be of service to the collective.

When you do write your intentions this New Moon, include practices that help you embrace your uniqueness. What can you do each day that helps you recognize your talents and release self-doubt? Often we need daily routines that help us nurture our gifts and give us an energetic boost to continue on our paths. Create rituals this New Moon that help you understand who you are and what you have to give others. Additionally, create practices that help you cultivate your gift each day so you feel more confident and empowered in giving them.

The habits we do daily with intent become the rituals of our lives. How you wake in the morning is a ritual. Having a pot of tea can be a ritual. Journaling is a ritual. These rituals become the foundation for your intentions to manifest. They keep the fire of your dreams burning long after the New Moon has passed and during even

VIRGO X NEW MOON

SEPTEMBER 6TH

the most distracting times. Rituals also help us define our time. Virgo reminds us that our time is finite and that we must treat it as a precious resource. Feel into what rituals can help you slowly build your visions. Virgo reminds us that we are in no rush to reach our destinations. The journey to our dreams is just as fulfilling as achieving them. What's important is that we create a strong foundation that will not waver in the face of adversity.

As you create and commit to rituals that will help you work toward your visions, include rituals of healing. Healing rituals look like daily journaling. They can be mantras you say when self-doubts arise. They may even be a plan for what to do when a certain thought or feeling comes up. This plan can include a breathing exercise, a series of questions to ask yourself, or a call to a loved one who can give you a different perspective. Virgo reminds us that our wounds can sabotage us in ways we least expect. If we want a strong foundation, we must heal the cracks in our souls. Unprocessed grief or trauma from the past creates energetic noise. It distracts us, takes us off course, and brings us out of the present moment. Our wounds can call in situations that repeat the past and cause chaos in our lives. Virgo is the sign of organization. It reminds us that to reach our highest visions, we must declutter our minds and hearts. Clean out your mind this New Moon as you would your closet. If it doesn't bring you joy, release it to make space for something that does.

Aspects

There are a few aspects this New Moon that affect the energy and add some new elements this year. The Moon and Sun trine Uranus Retrograde in Taurus. Trines mean the cosmic bodies are 120° away from each other in the sky. They are harmonious aspects and merge the energy in a complementary way. Uranus is the planet of change and innovation. It asks us to use a different lens to think of new solutions to old problems. Stationed retrograde, Uranus brings this energy of change inward and asks us to shift our inner landscape. We often resist the change Uranus asks of us, and we can feel like we are having an internal meltdown as this energy challenges our old patterns.

Eventually, though, we break through to a new perspective, and what was once a staple of our existence becomes a thing of the past. Uranus's energy works on old thoughts, outdated viewpoints, and even emotions that have run their course. Uranus Retrograde has the power to help us change anything about ourselves and become someone we once couldn't even imagine.

With this energy feeding into the New Moon, we have the opportunity to break free of habits that no longer serve us. We may also encounter situations around this New Moon that force us to change for the better even though it may be an uncomfortable process. With Uranus involved this New Moon, it's better to let go with grace while you have the choice. Change comes with this energy, so expect the unexpected and know that it's all meant to help you own your magic.

Harness the energy of change this New Moon to shift the way you think about perfection. Perfection leaves no room for growth or learning. It doesn't allow for forgiveness or compassion. It also takes away time that you could spend on something else instead of attempting to perfect something. Plus, perfection is not necessary for a happy life. Everyone has something that makes them imperfect. We all have flaws, and those flaws are what make us unique. Imperfections not only make you real, they make you special—and they should be honored this New Moon. Align with Uranus Retrograde to change the way you think about your imperfections. Instead of seeing them as something that makes you not good enough, see them as something that makes you unique and worthy of acceptance, love, and recognition.

SETTING UP FOR MAGIC

Each zodiac sign carries inherent energy. With this energy come colors, shapes, scents, and elements that match its vibration. For every New Moon, we want to incorporate as many of these frequencies as possible. While none of them is required to align with the energy of the New Moon, they do help reflect the energy. Think of them as energetic mirrors placed around the room to amplify and direct the energy. Use your intuition to guide the choice and placement of objects. Resist the urge to overthink where they belong. Let the crystals, in particular, choose their location; all you need to do is listen.

Pick a space that feels centered and stable, either inside or outside. Your circle should feel protected and safe. It also needs to be relatively quiet and free of distracting noises. For this Virgo New Moon, practice near the Earth if possible. If you can't practice outside, bring the Earth inside through flowers, plants, and crystals.

Once you designate a space for your circle, imagine a white light creating the boundary. Place a crystal, candle, or another piece of magic in the center to give structure to the circle. This center is also where you can set up a crystal grid to help further direct the energy. For Virgo, create a crystal grid in the shape of a star, hexagon, or pentagon. Earth crystal grids have a structured shape to them that helps bring grounding, order, and clarity to the space. If available, place a generator, or tower crystal, in the center. These crystals have six sides and amplify the other crystals in the grid.

If you are creating an altar, place it in the easterly corner to help call in the energy of new beginnings. You can adorn your altar with images that inspire new beginnings. You can also place images of your mentors and teachers, as the energy of mentorship belongs to Virgo and the Sixth House. You can also place on your altar flowers, crystals, jewelry, or other treasures that remind you of your journey, power, and potential. After you write your intentions, they can rest here as well.

After your altar and circle's center are in place, position other objects around the circle to anchor the four directions. You can also place magical items at key places in

SETTING UP FOR MAGIC

the circle, such as near the doorway for protection, or if a section feels energetically off in some way. You can use candles, crystals, flowers, plants, bowls of water, and anything else that feels special to you. Incorporate all the elements if possible, feeling supported in your work by all of them.

Know that your attention and awareness of the power available is the most important thing for working with it. You can practice the exercises in this workbook in any way you choose; you can practice alone, on a train, or in a group of people around a bonfire. Your willingness to open up, look within, and expand your consciousness is the most essential piece to this day.

The other pieces for calling in and aligning with the energy of Virgo are listed in the box below on this page. You can combine them any way you like.

Once you've set up your circle, cleanse it through a purification ritual using a bundled dried herb like lavender or rosemary. Cleanse in the easternmost point of the circle and make your way around the circle in a clockwise direction. Know that as you cleanse the circle, you are also creating a container for the energy of the night. After the circle is cleansed, cleanse yourself and your friends before they enter the circle by waving the dried herb bundle from head to toe, encasing the whole body with smoke.

You can begin the circle by acknowledging everyone in the room. Have everyone introduce themselves and share their sign, their favorite flower, or some other piece of information that connects the circle. You can then continue to the yoga if you are practicing, and then the meditation. Once you feel the room is centered, talk about the astrology of the night and what it means for each of you. If it is a larger circle, you may want to designate a talking stick or crystal that each guest holds while they speak.

After you've shared your understandings, continue with the questions and the journaling portion of this workbook. After everyone has finished, talk again about your experiences with the energy and the revelations that may have occurred. You can share as little or as much as you like with the group. Never feel obligated to speak; sometimes energies need time to develop before they are brought to the light of day. At this point, you may also pull some cards to help tune further into your intuitive guidance. You can use manifestation cards, oracle cards, tarot cards, goddess cards, animal medicine cards, or any other decks in your toolkit.

Once you've finished the circle, close it by having everyone shut their eyes and meditate on what they are grateful for that night and every night. You can even practice being grateful for things that haven't come your way yet. Gratitude will attract them to your energetic field and let the Universe know you are ready to receive them. Enjoy this time to be with your self, your heart, and your soul. Get to know yourself on a deeper level and allow your life to unfold another layer each New Moon.

FOR YOUR ALTAR OR MOON CIRCLE

FLOWERS:
Chrysanthemums, Ivy, Hyacinth, & Buttercups

COLORS:
Dark Greens, Tans, & Browns

TEXTURES/FABRIC:
Medium Woods

SCENTS:
Rosemary, Lavender, & Sandalwood

SHAPES:
Rectangles & Hexagons

ELEMENTS:
Plants, Flowers, Herbs

Lessons from Virgo:

- You have something unique to offer the world.

- Only you are in charge of your life.

- Imperfections make you real.

- You are already enough.

- spirit daughter

NEW MOON QUESTIONS

These questions are designed to help you become clear in your intentions. Take a few deep breaths to ground yourself before answering them. Sit with each question for a moment and allow the answer to naturally arise, being open to the person you are becoming. As you write, know you are opening the door to your intuition and giving permission to your highest visions to come out and be seen.

1. How does perfectionism and self-doubt play in a role in your life? Does it block you or prevent you from manifesting your magic?

2. What helps you feel good enough and worthy of love and acceptance? How can you nourish these things and include more of them daily in your life?

3. What unique gift do you hold for the world? How do you give this gift? How can you allow yourself to step into its power even more?

4. If you allowed yourself to be imperfect, what would you do? Who would you be? What chances would you take?

INTENTION SETTING

Now is the time to plant your intentions for this lunar cycle. Some of these intentions will come to fruition by the next Full Moon; others will come into your world over the next six months—by the Full Moon in Virgo. You can also plant intentions that go far into the future. Your intentions help you call in the vibrations you need to manifest your dreams. Some intentions will usher in new behaviors, while others will bring you new experiences and opportunities for growth that will propel your path forward.

On the Virgo New Moon, it's most beneficial to create intentions around your gifts and unique offerings to the world. These intentions can include seeing your perfection and worth. See yourself showing up fully in your power, giving your gifts to the world to help it heal and evolve. Include seeing yourself grounded and connected to your body, ready to take charge of your life. Also, envision healthy boundaries around your space and time—boundaries that allow for your self-care. Include different rituals that will help you build your visions over time. Remember, with Virgo it's a slow and steady course. Patience and commitment are key.

Take a moment to create a scene in your mind. In this scene, all that you wish to call in is already yours. All you desire to change has already occurred. Do not worry about how you will get there or the list of to-dos needed to accomplish your goals. Just focus on the feeling of already living your dream. Know with every ounce of your being that it is already true; it already exists for you. Also, know that your intuition, not your logic, will lead you to this dream.

Write with as much detail as possible and without limits. Just let your mind explore. Align with the energy of Virgo to clarify your dreams. What does your envisioned life feel like? How does this dream make you feel? What emotions does it bring up? As you write, feel a sense of gratitude for what you are dreaming; thank the Universe for giving it to you and thank yourself for creating it. Gratitude always creates abundance.

_____

_____

_____

_____

_____

_____

_____

_____

_____

_____

INTENTION SETTING

NEW MOON AFFIRMATIONS

The New Moon is a powerful day for diving inward to your most hidden subconscious thoughts and patterns. In this space, you'll find the programs that are directing your life behind the scenes—most of the time without you even knowing. You can look to the house in which this New Moon falls for you to find some guidance on which area of your life these mantras might show up. For instance, if Virgo rules your Seventh House, look for programing around your relationships. What do you tell yourself about these things daily? Below, write down your old programming. These can be things like "I'll never be good enough," "It's too hard," "I must try harder," or "I'm not capable." Then rewrite your old mantras into new ones that oppose and challenge the old ones. Repeat your new affirmations daily until the next New Moon. Repetition is the key to new programming.

OLD PROGRAMMING

NEW PROGRAMMING

PERSONAL SIGNS

DISCERNMENT. PATIENCE. KIND-HEARTEDNESS. SERVICE.

At their best, people with their Sun in Virgo are highly intuitive healers capable of great understanding and empathy. They live in service of others and find fulfillment in this role. They take great care to perfect their offering to the world and succeed once they learn to love themselves unconditionally.

Virgos have both the fortunate and unfortunate ability to see their greatness. They know their potential, and they set out arbitrary points to let them know if they are reaching that potential. Simply put, Virgos know how perfect life can be. This

PERSONAL SIGNS

knowledge can do two things for Virgos: it can drive them mad as they try to achieve this unobtainable goal, or it can inspire them to focus on the journey and enjoy the climb to the top of a mountain they may never reach. The choice is theirs. Once they realize they will never obtain perfection, they become free to enjoy an imperfect life full of opportunity for growth. They start living and stop focusing on mistakes or regrets. Not all Virgos can reach this type of enlightenment. Those who do, though, empower themselves and others to live a life full of joy, healing, and evolution.

Virgos are powerful healers, both for themselves and others. They have a natural gift for knowing what needs to shift in someone's energy for them to feel whole once again. They possess an unparalleled skill of discernment and can quickly see the pieces of any puzzle. Where someone else may view an issue as a tangled web, Virgos can precisely pick apart the pieces and handle each one with grace and inner knowing. Once they learn to accept their gift, they can break down complex issues into bite-sized information others can digest. They also need to understand that their talents are good enough to give to others. Every Virgo needs to practice radical self-acceptance to increase their sense of worthiness to step into their true power.

Once a Virgo sees the beauty of their existence, they are ready to be of service and, more importantly, teach. Virgo is the sign of mentorship. They are the teachers of the world and have much to offer the collective. They see things others cannot understand. They also have a capacity for patience, which is a critical skill for any teacher. Virgos need to refine their patience through time in nature, where patience is expected. As they ground their energy and find their natural, unrushed rhythm, they can become the wise mentor they have always looked for but have never found. They become their own teacher.

People with their Moon in Virgo need to feel needed. They enjoy being of service to others and go out of their way to help people reach their goals. They find genuine fulfillment when nourishing others. They also need to be appreciated for their efforts and often look for validation from others. While appreciation is a bond-building energy, Virgo Moons need to learn to appreciate themselves. They need to feel good enough and of value without anyone else telling them they are. This realization requires a lifetime of self-development and understanding.

Virgo Moons are best when they are working on themselves. They enjoy growth in all areas and energetically stagnate when not challenged. They are always trying to improve themselves, especially emotionally. They must be careful to not get caught up in perfectionism, and they must understand that growth is a journey, not a destination. They will always have more to learn and more to uncover. This is what makes life interesting and enjoyable.

In matters of the heart, Virgo Moons can be a bit emotionally detached. They are highly technical and discerning, and they can view love as an equation to solve instead of a magical journey of the heart. They need to find someone who pushes them out of their logical mind and encourages them to feel. Emotions can be uncomfortable for Virgo Moons because they always like to stay in control. But those emotions can also be freeing. Once a Virgo Moon finds the person who can open their heart, they have no trouble committing because this Earth sign loves stability.

ASTROLOGY FORECAST

AUGUST 30TH - SEPTEMBER 20TH

Aug. 30: Last Quarter in Gemini

Today we begin the final phase of this lunar cycle, the Last Quarter, which takes place in the energy of Gemini. It's a time to fearlessly question all the elements of your world. If the answers do not align with your vision and potential, then allow this waning Air Moon to sweep them away. Gemini is the energy of inspiration. It inspires us to be curious about everything. It also inspires us to be creative in our search for the truth.

When the Last Quarter is in Gemini, feel into your truths. Ask the hard questions about where you're going and how you're going to get there. Look over all the pieces of the puzzle that make up your life. Do they all fit? Look over the stories you tell yourself. Are they all true? Spend time with this energy as you survey your land and make changes where needed. Feel your heightened ability to make decisions today and use it to prepare yourself for the New Moon next week.

Aug. 30: Mercury enters Libra

Mercury, the planet of communication, enters the balanced energy of Libra today until November 5 due to a retrograde beginning September 26. Mercury in Libra inspires us to have conversations with our partners. It's time to both listen and speak your truth as the airwaves open to understanding. Over this transit, focus on feeling peace and balance within before speaking to another. Once you've reached a state of calmness in your own energy, encourage your partner to do the same. Then focus on an equal exchange of energy between the two of you, with room for thoughts to unfold and feelings to land. Hold space for one another and encourage a deep connection with your breath as you communicate. Take this time to nurture your relationship through balanced communication that allows you both to feel heard.

Sept. 10: Venus enters Scorpio

Venus is the planet of love and beauty. Today she enters Scorpio's energy until October 7, reminding us of the power of love and its ability to heal. Venus inspires compassion, and with Scorpio's energy, she grants us the opportunity to heal old wounds around femininity. Venus in Scorpio is a time to align with your wild feminine—untamed by the constructs of the world we live in. Feel the power of your femininity. Feel its ability to nurture, heal, inspire, create, and make you passionate about life.

ASTROLOGY FORECAST

AUGUST 30TH - SEPTEMBER 20TH

Sept. 13: First Quarter in Sagittarius

Today the Moon makes it one quarter through the lunar cycle, squaring the Sun and creating a half moon as she builds. On one side we have the Sun in Virgo asking for structure and order. On the other, we have Sagittarius, who seeks to destroy all walls for the sake of full expansion. The First Quarter Moon is a time when our first blocks pop up around the intentions we set on the New Moon. Most of these barriers are internal though, meaning we control them.

Virgo seeks to define. As an Earth sign, this energy inspires us to create containers in our lives. These can be schedules, time to work on our healing, and, yes, even days spent organizing a closet. Sagittarius knows no containers. This energy inspires us to take leaps of faith, seek new adventures, and use new truths to burn down old ways of thinking.

As you work with both of these energies today, ask yourself how you can stay grounded while expanding your horizons. How can you use your containers of time and space to venture into unknown territory instead of preventing your evolution? We often think of schedules as limiting. Organization, though, can actually bring us freedom as long as we remain flexible. It's like taking a well-planned trip while leaving room for serendipity and finding silver linings if things get canceled. Today, feel into how you can merge the vibrations of Sagittarius and Virgo to create steps toward your visions, staying focused while inviting in the unimaginable.

Sept. 14: Mars enters Libra

Mars, the planet of passion, enters the calming vibrations of Libra until October 30. Mars in Libra encourages us to think about our relations in contrast to the soul's passions. It asks if our partners are supporting us or causing us to create wars within ourselves. This transit can cause heated discussions with people in your life, so use caution when discussing important topics. Calm the warrior within you and know that your words will land more effectively if they come from a place of peace instead of frustration.

Sept. 20: Full Moon in Pisces

Please refer to the Pisces Full Moon Workbook.

UP NEXT
LIBRA SEASON

SEPTEMBER 22ND

Prepare to find harmony in your relationships and inner world, as we fall into the energy of balance and beauty with Libra Season.

PURCHASE AT SPIRITDAUGHTER.COM

HAPPY NEW MOON!

Thank you to everyone who supported and purchased this workbook.

Special Thanks to Rebecca Reitz (rebeccareitz.com, @becca_reitz) for her beautiful artwork on the cover, page 2, 4, 6, 14, 16, 28.

For a monthly subscription contact hello@spiritdaughter.com
or visit www.spiritdaughter.com.

Disclaimer: The exercises and yoga sequences in this book are physical activities that should be performed carefully to avoid injury. You agree to accept all risks and release Spirit Daughter and any guest instructors from any and all liabilities. Please take care and enjoy.

Follow along our journey on IG:
@spiritdaughter

We always love seeing your photos & hearing about your experiences with the workbooks! Tag us to be featured on our community page:
@spiritdaughtercollective